The Ultimate Money Move for Teenagers:

Saving Strategies & Growing Your Money Smartly

By Asher Bennett

All rights reserved. No part of this publication may be reproduced, distributed, or transmitted in any form or by any means, including photocopying, recording, or other electronic or mechanical methods, without the prior written permission of the publisher, except in the case of brief quotations embodied in critical reviews and certain other noncommercial uses permitted by copyright law.

Copyright © (Asher Bennett), (2024).

Table Of Contents

Introduction

Setting Financial Goals

Budgeting Basics

Earning Money

Saving Smart

Investing 101

Managing Money Wisely

Financial Tools and Apps: Best Apps for Budgeting and Saving

The Importance of Financial Literacy

Dealing with Financial Challenges

Planning for the Future

Giving Back

Case Studies and Real-Life Examples

Conclusion

Introduction

In today's fast-paced world, financial independence is an essential goal for individuals of all ages. For teenagers, understanding and striving for financial independence is particularly crucial as it sets the foundation for a secure and prosperous future. This introduction will delve into the concept of financial independence, why it matters for teenagers, and how it can significantly impact their lives.

Understanding Financial Independence

What is Financial Independence?

Financial independence means having sufficient personal wealth to live without having to work actively for basic necessities. For teenagers, this doesn't imply being entirely self-sufficient right away but rather learning to manage money wisely and build habits that will lead to financial security in adulthood.

Building Blocks of Financial Independence

1. Income Generation: The first step toward financial independence is understanding how to generate income. This can be through part-time jobs, internships, freelance work, or entrepreneurial ventures. It's essential for teenagers to learn the value of work and how it translates into financial gain.

2. Budgeting: Creating and maintaining a budget helps track income and expenses, ensuring that money is managed wisely. Budgeting teaches teenagers to prioritise needs over wants and make informed financial decisions.

3. Saving: Saving money is a critical habit that lays the groundwork for financial independence. Encouraging teenagers to set aside a portion of their earnings fosters a mindset of preparing for the future.

4. Investing: While investing might seem complex, it's a powerful tool for growing wealth. teenagers who learn the basics of investing can start small and gradually build a portfolio that generates passive income.

5. Debt Management: Understanding how to handle debt responsibly is crucial. teenagers should learn about the implications of borrowing and the importance of maintaining a good credit score.

Why Money Matters for teenagers

Early Financial Literacy

Learning about money management at a young age equips teenagers with the skills they need to navigate the financial world. Early financial literacy has been linked to better financial behaviours in adulthood. According to a study by the Financial Industry Regulatory Authority (FINRA), young adults who received financial education were more likely to have savings and retirement accounts and less likely to incur high-cost debt.

Building Confidence and Independence

Understanding and managing money instils confidence in teenagers. It empowers them to make informed decisions and fosters a sense of independence. When teenagers know how to handle their finances, they are less likely to rely on others for financial support, giving them a sense of autonomy and control over their lives.

Preparing for Future Responsibilities

teenagers who learn about money early are better prepared for the financial responsibilities that come with adulthood. This includes paying for college, buying a car, renting an apartment, and eventually purchasing a home. By understanding financial principles, they can make decisions that align with their long-term goals and avoid common pitfalls.

Preventing Financial Mistakes

Financial mistakes can have long-lasting consequences. By educating teenagers about money management, we can help them avoid common errors such as overspending, accruing excessive debt, and falling victim to scams. Knowledgeable teenagers are more likely to navigate financial challenges successfully and build a solid financial foundation.

Encouraging a Healthy Relationship with Money

A healthy relationship with money involves understanding its value and using it as a tool to achieve goals rather than as a source of stress or anxiety. Teaching teenagers about money helps them develop a balanced perspective, where they can enjoy the benefits of their earnings while also planning for the future.

Practical Steps for teenagers to Achieve Financial Independence

1. Start Earning Early

Encourage teenagers to find part-time jobs or engage in side hustles. Whether it's babysitting, tutoring, or working at a local store, earning money provides valuable lessons in responsibility and time management. Moreover, it gives them firsthand experience in handling income and expenses.

2. Learn to Budget

Budgeting is a fundamental skill for financial independence. teenagers should be taught to track their income and expenses, categorise their spending, and identify areas where they can save. Numerous apps and online tools can help make budgeting easier and more engaging for young people.

3. Emphasise the Importance of Saving

Saving money should be a priority from an early age. Encourage teenagers to set savings goals, whether it's for a new gadget, a car, or college tuition. Opening a savings account and regularly contributing to it instills a habit of saving and highlights the benefits of compound interest over time.

4. Introduce Basic Investing Concepts

Investing can seem daunting, but starting with the basics can demystify the process. Teach teenagers about different investment options, such as stocks, bonds, and mutual funds. Consider using educational platforms or simulated stock market games to provide practical experience without financial risk.

5. Teach Responsible Debt Management

Understanding debt and how to manage it is crucial. Explain the difference between good debt (such as student loans or a mortgage) and bad debt (like high-interest credit card debt). Emphasise the importance of paying off debts on time and maintaining a good credit score.

6. Encourage Financial Education

Financial literacy is an ongoing journey. Encourage teenagers to seek out resources such as books, online courses, and financial blogs. Schools and community organisations often offer financial education programs that can provide valuable insights and guidance.

Long-Term Benefits of Financial Independence

1. Greater Career Flexibility

teenagers who achieve financial independence early in life have greater career flexibility. They can pursue careers that align with their passions rather than feeling pressured to take high-paying jobs to meet immediate financial needs. Financial security allows for more thoughtful career choices and can lead to greater job satisfaction.

2. Enhanced Quality of Life

Financial independence contributes to a higher quality of life. It reduces stress and anxiety related to money and provides the freedom to make choices that align with personal values and goals. Financially independent individuals can enjoy experiences and opportunities that may be out of reach for those struggling with financial instability.

3. Ability to Give Back

Financially secure individuals are in a better position to give back to their communities. Whether through charitable donations, volunteering, or supporting loved ones, financial independence enables teenagers to make a positive impact on the world around them.

4. Long-Term Financial Security

Building habits of saving, investing, and responsible spending sets the stage for long-term financial security. teenagers who start early are more likely to accumulate wealth, achieve financial goals, and enjoy a comfortable retirement.

5. Empowerment and Self-Reliance

Achieving financial independence empowers teenagers to take control of their lives. It fosters self-reliance and confidence, knowing they have the skills and resources to navigate financial challenges and opportunities.

Conclusion

Understanding financial independence and why money matters are essential lessons for teenagers. By equipping young people with the knowledge and skills to manage their finances, we set them on a path toward a secure and prosperous future. The journey to financial independence begins with education, practical experience, and the development of healthy financial habits. As teenagers learn to earn, budget, save, invest, and manage debt, they gain the confidence and independence needed to navigate the financial landscape of adulthood successfully.

Setting Financial Goals

Setting financial goals is a fundamental step toward achieving financial stability and independence. These goals provide direction, motivation, and a clear pathway to managing money effectively. In this discussion, we will explore the difference between short-term and long-term financial goals and how to create a financial roadmap to achieve these goals.

Short-Term vs. Long-Term Goals

Short-Term Goals

Short-term financial goals are objectives that can be achieved within a relatively short period, typically within a year. These goals are often more immediate and easier to attain compared to long-term goals. Examples include:

1. Building an Emergency Fund: Setting aside money for unexpected expenses, such as medical bills or car repairs, can prevent financial stress.
2. Paying Off Small Debts: Reducing or eliminating small credit card balances or personal loans can improve financial health and increase disposable income.
3. Saving for a Vacation: Allocating funds for a planned trip can make the experience more enjoyable without the burden of debt.
4. Purchasing a New Gadget: Saving up for the latest smartphone or laptop ensures you can buy it outright without using credit.

Achieving these short-term goals requires specific, actionable steps and disciplined savings or repayment strategies. They often serve as the foundation for building good financial habits that will support long-term goals.

Long-Term Goals

Long-term financial goals require more time and effort to achieve, typically spanning several years or even decades. These goals are crucial for securing financial stability and ensuring a comfortable future. Examples include:

1. Saving for Retirement: Building a retirement fund through investments in 401(k) plans, IRAs, or other retirement accounts ensures financial security in later years.
2. Buying a Home: Accumulating enough savings for a down payment and securing a mortgage are significant milestones for homeownership.
3. Funding Education: Saving for college tuition or other educational expenses can provide opportunities for personal and professional growth.
4. Building Wealth: Investing in stocks, bonds, or real estate to grow net worth over time can lead to financial independence and the ability to live comfortably without relying on active income.

Long-term goals require careful planning, consistent effort, and often involve making strategic financial decisions that align with one's future aspirations.

Creating a Financial Roadmap

A financial roadmap is a comprehensive plan that outlines the steps needed to achieve both short-term and long-term financial goals. Here's how to create an effective financial roadmap:

1. Assess Your Current Financial Situation

Before setting goals, it's essential to understand your current financial status. This involves:

- Calculating Net Worth: List all assets (e.g., savings, investments, property) and liabilities (e.g., debts, loans) to determine your net worth.
- Evaluating Income and Expenses: Track your monthly income and expenses to identify areas where you can save or cut costs.

2. Define Clear, Specific Goals

Your financial goals should be SMART: Specific, Measurable, Achievable, Relevant, and Time-bound. For example:

- Specific: Instead of saying "I want to save money," specify "I want to save $5,000 for an emergency fund."
- Measurable: Ensure you can track progress. For example, "I will save $200 per month."
- Achievable: Set realistic goals based on your financial situation.
- Relevant: Align your goals with your overall financial objectives.
- Time-bound: Set a deadline for achieving your goals.

3. Prioritize Your Goals

Not all goals have the same level of urgency or importance. Prioritise your goals based on factors such as:

- Urgency: Some goals, like building an emergency fund, might be more urgent than others.

- Impact: Consider the long-term benefits of achieving a particular goal. For instance, saving for retirement might have a more significant impact on your future financial security than saving for a vacation.

4. Create a Budget

A budget is a crucial tool for managing your finances and achieving your goals. Follow these steps to create an effective budget:

- Track Income and Expenses: Record all sources of income and categorise your expenses (e.g., housing, utilities, food, entertainment).
- Set Spending Limits: Allocate a specific amount to each expense category and stick to these limits.
- Include Savings: Treat savings as a mandatory expense. Allocate a portion of your income to savings and investments each month.

5. Develop a Savings and Investment Plan

Saving and investing are key components of achieving financial goals. Consider the following strategies:

- Emergency Fund: Aim to save three to six months' worth of living expenses in a readily accessible account.
- Retirement Savings: Contribute to retirement accounts such as a 401(k) or IRA. Take advantage of employer matching contributions if available.
- Investing: Diversify your investments across different asset classes (e.g., stocks, bonds, real estate) to manage risk and maximise returns.

6. Monitor and Adjust Your Plan

Regularly review your financial roadmap to ensure you are on track to achieve your goals. Make adjustments as needed based on changes in your financial situation or priorities. This might involve:

- Reassessing Goals: If your income increases, you might set more ambitious goals. Conversely, if unexpected expenses arise, you might need to adjust your savings targets.
- Adjusting Budget: Modify your budget to reflect changes in income or expenses. For example, if you pay off a debt, you might allocate the freed-up funds to savings or other goals.
- Rebalancing Investments: Periodically review your investment portfolio to ensure it aligns with your risk tolerance and financial objectives.

7. Seek Professional Advice

Consider consulting a financial advisor for personalised guidance and to help you navigate complex financial decisions. A professional can provide valuable insights and strategies tailored to your unique circumstances and goals.

Conclusion

Setting financial goals and creating a financial roadmap are essential steps toward achieving financial independence and security. By distinguishing between short-term and long-term goals, individuals can prioritize their efforts and develop a clear plan for managing their finances effectively. Through disciplined budgeting, saving, investing, and regular monitoring, anyone can work towards their financial aspirations and build a stable, prosperous future.

Understanding the importance of financial planning and taking proactive steps to manage money can lead to significant long-term benefits, including greater career flexibility, enhanced quality of life, and the ability to give back to the community. Ultimately, a well-crafted financial roadmap serves as a valuable guide on the journey to financial success and independence.

Budgeting Basics

Budgeting is a fundamental aspect of personal finance management. It involves creating a plan for how to spend your money, ensuring that your income covers your expenses and helps you achieve your financial goals. This guide will cover the importance of budgeting and provide a step-by-step approach to creating and sticking to a budget.

The Importance of Budgeting

1. Financial Control and Awareness

Budgeting gives you control over your finances by providing a clear picture of your income and expenses. It helps you understand where your money is going and enables you to make informed financial decisions. According to a study by the National Foundation for Credit Counseling, individuals who create a budget are more likely to feel in control of their finances and less stressed about money.

2. Goal Achievement

A budget helps you allocate funds towards specific financial goals, whether they are short-term (e.g., saving for a vacation) or long-term (e.g., building a retirement fund). By setting aside money regularly, you can systematically work towards achieving these goals.

3. Avoiding Debt

Budgeting helps prevent overspending and the accumulation of debt. By tracking your expenses and living within your means, you can avoid relying on credit cards or loans to cover your daily needs. This reduces financial stress and improves your overall financial health.

4. Emergency Preparedness

An effective budget includes an emergency fund, which is crucial for handling unexpected expenses like medical bills, car repairs, or job loss. According to a report by the Federal Reserve, 40% of Americans would struggle to cover a $400 emergency expense without borrowing or selling something. Having an emergency fund can provide financial security and peace of mind.

5. Improved Saving and Investment

Budgeting helps you identify areas where you can cut costs and increase your savings. By regularly saving and investing, you can build wealth over time and achieve financial independence.

How to Create and Stick to a Budget

1. Assess Your Income

The first step in creating a budget is to determine your total monthly income. This includes your salary, bonuses, freelance work, and any other sources of income. Make sure to calculate your net income (after taxes) to understand how much money you actually have to work with.

2. Track Your Expenses

Identify and categorise your monthly expenses. This typically includes:

- Fixed Expenses: These are regular, consistent payments such as rent or mortgage, utilities, insurance, and loan payments.
- Variable Expenses: These fluctuate each month and include groceries, transportation, entertainment, dining out, and clothing.
- Discretionary Expenses: These are non-essential expenses such as hobbies, subscriptions, and luxury items.

To get an accurate picture, track your spending for at least one month. Use bank statements, receipts, and budgeting apps to record every expense.

3. Set Financial Goals

Determine your short-term and long-term financial goals. Short-term goals might include saving for a vacation or paying off a small debt, while long-term goals could be buying a home, saving for retirement, or funding education. Be specific about the amount of money you need and the timeline for achieving each goal.

4. Create a Budget Plan

Allocate your income to different expense categories and financial goals. A common budgeting method is the 50/30/20 rule:

- 50% for Needs: Essential expenses such as housing, utilities, groceries, transportation, and healthcare.
- 30% for Wants: Discretionary spending on dining out, entertainment, hobbies, and non-essential items.

- 20% for Savings and Debt Repayment: Contributions to savings accounts, investments, and paying down debt.

Adjust these percentages based on your personal financial situation and goals. The key is to ensure that your total expenses do not exceed your income.

5. Implement and Monitor Your Budget

Once your budget is created, implement it by tracking your spending against your budgeted amounts. Use budgeting apps or spreadsheets to make this process easier. Regularly review your budget to ensure you are staying on track and adjust as necessary. Monitoring your budget helps you identify any areas where you might be overspending and allows you to make timely corrections.

6. Adjust and Improve

Your budget should be flexible to accommodate changes in your financial situation or goals. If you receive a raise, for example, allocate the extra income towards your savings or debt repayment. Conversely, if your expenses increase, adjust your discretionary spending to stay within your budget.

7. Stick to Your Budget

Sticking to a budget requires discipline and consistency. Here are some tips to help you adhere to your budget:

- Automate Savings: Set up automatic transfers to your savings or investment accounts to ensure you save regularly without thinking about it.

- Limit Discretionary Spending: Identify areas where you can cut back on non-essential expenses. For example, reduce dining out or cancel unused subscriptions.
- Use Cash for Variable Expenses: Withdraw cash for categories like groceries and entertainment. When the cash is gone, you know you've reached your limit.
- Track Progress: Regularly review your financial goals and progress. Celebrate milestones to stay motivated.
- Seek Support: Share your budgeting goals with a friend or family member who can help hold you accountable.

Conclusion

Budgeting is a powerful tool for managing your finances, achieving your goals, and securing your financial future. By understanding the importance of budgeting and following a structured approach to create and stick to a budget, you can take control of your financial life. Regularly reviewing and adjusting your budget ensures that it remains relevant and effective in helping you achieve your financial objectives. Whether you are saving for an emergency fund, paying off debt, or investing for the future, a well-planned budget is the foundation of financial success.

Earning Money

Earning money as a teenager can provide valuable life lessons, build a sense of responsibility, and set the stage for future financial independence. There are various ways for teenagers to earn money, ranging from traditional part-time jobs to entrepreneurial ventures. Here, we will explore both options in detail.

Part-Time Jobs and Gigs

1. Retail and Food Service Jobs

Working in retail or food service is a common choice for teenagers. These jobs offer flexible hours, especially during weekends and holidays, and teach essential customer service skills. Examples include:

- Cashier or Sales Associate: Working at local stores or malls.
- Waitstaff or Busser: Serving customers in restaurants or cafes.
- Barista: Making coffee and other beverages at coffee shops.

2. Babysitting

Babysitting is a popular gig for teenagers who enjoy working with children. It offers flexible hours and can be quite lucrative, especially if the teen is reliable and builds a good reputation. Websites like Care.com and UrbanSitter can help teenagers find babysitting jobs.

3. Tutoring

teenagers who excel in academic subjects can offer tutoring services to younger students. This can be done in person or online through platforms like Wyzant and Tutor.com. Tutoring not only helps earn money but also reinforces the tutor's own knowledge and skills.

4. Lawn Care and Landscaping

Providing lawn care services, such as mowing lawns, raking leaves, and planting flowers, can be a great way for teenagers to earn money, especially in neighbourhoods. This job promotes physical activity and teaches responsibility.

5. Pet Sitting and Dog Walking

For animal lovers, pet sitting and dog walking are excellent ways to earn money. Websites like Rover.com connect pet owners with pet sitters and dog walkers, offering flexible job opportunities.

6. Freelancing

teenagers with skills in graphic design, writing, or coding can take on freelance gigs. Platforms like Fiverr and Upwork allow teenagers to offer their services to a global market. This not only helps them earn money but also builds a professional portfolio.

7. Seasonal Jobs

Many businesses hire extra help during busy seasons, such as summer camps, amusement parks, and holiday retail. These jobs are perfect for teenagers looking to earn money during school breaks.

Entrepreneurial Ventures for teenagers

1. Online Businesses

The internet offers numerous opportunities for entrepreneurial teenagers to start their own businesses. Examples include:

- E-commerce: Selling handmade crafts, vintage items, or drop-shipped products on platforms like Etsy, eBay, or Shopify.
- Print-on-Demand: Creating custom designs for t-shirts, mugs, and other items sold through websites like Teespring and Redbubble.

2. Blogging and Vlogging

teenagers passionate about a particular subject can start a blog or YouTube channel. By consistently creating quality content, they can attract a following and monetize their site through ads, sponsorships, and affiliate marketing. Blogging platforms like WordPress and video-sharing sites like YouTube provide tools and resources to get started.

3. Social Media Management

With a knack for social media, teenagers can offer their services to small businesses to manage their social media accounts. This involves creating content, scheduling posts, and engaging with followers. Knowledge of platforms like Instagram, Facebook, and Twitter is essential.

4. Creating and Selling Crafts

teenagers who are creative can make and sell crafts, such as jewellery, candles, or artwork. Local craft fairs, farmers' markets, and online marketplaces like Etsy are great venues for selling handmade items.

5. Lawn Care Business

Starting a lawn care business can be more than just a gig; it can become a regular source of income. By investing in basic equipment and marketing their services, teenagers can grow a steady client base in their community.

6. Car Wash Services

Setting up a mobile car wash service is another entrepreneurial venture. teenagers can offer to wash and detail cars at the customer's location, providing convenience and personalised service.

7. Event Planning and Assistance

For teenagers with organisational skills, offering event planning or assistance services for parties, weddings, and other gatherings can be a profitable venture. This can involve tasks like setting up venues, decorating, and managing schedules.

8. Customised Apparel and Accessories

Using tools like heat presses and embroidery machines, teenagers can create customised apparel and accessories. They can market their products through social media and local events.

9. Baking and Cooking

For those who enjoy baking or cooking, making and selling homemade treats or meals can be a fun and profitable business. Selling at local farmers' markets or taking custom orders from friends and family can help get the business off the ground.

10. Personal Training or Coaching

teenagers with a passion for fitness or sports can offer personal training or coaching services to younger kids or peers. This can include fitness training, specific sports coaching, or even dance classes.

Conclusion

Earning money as a teen through part-time jobs or entrepreneurial ventures provides valuable life lessons and financial benefits. Whether choosing traditional jobs or starting a business, teenagers can develop skills that will serve them well throughout their lives. By exploring different opportunities and finding what best suits their interests and abilities, teenagers can take significant steps toward financial independence and personal growth.

Saving Smart

Saving money is a crucial aspect of financial planning that can provide security, flexibility, and peace of mind. This section will explore the importance of saving early and how to choose the right savings account.

The Power of Saving Early

1. Compound Interest

One of the most compelling reasons to start saving early is the benefit of compound interest. Compound interest is the interest earned on both the initial principal and the accumulated interest from previous periods. The longer your money is invested, the more you can benefit from this effect.

For example, if you save $1,000 at an annual interest rate of 5%, you will have $1,050 after one year. In the second year, you will earn interest not just on the $1,000, but on the $1,050, resulting in $1,102.50. Over time, this exponential growth can significantly increase your savings.

2. Financial Security

Starting to save early helps build a financial cushion that can provide security in times of need. An emergency fund, typically covering three to six months of living expenses, can help you manage unexpected expenses such as medical bills, car repairs, or job loss without going into debt.

3. Achieving Financial Goals

Whether it's buying a house, travelling, or funding education, starting to save early allows you to systematically work towards your financial goals. The earlier you start, the less you need to save each month to reach your target, thanks to the time value of money.

4. Habit Formation

Developing the habit of saving early in life sets a strong foundation for financial discipline. It encourages budgeting, careful spending, and prioritising financial well-being over impulsive purchases.

5. Retirement Planning

The earlier you start saving for retirement, the more time your investments have to grow. Even small contributions made consistently over time can result in a substantial retirement fund, reducing the need for large contributions later in life.

Choosing the Right Savings Account

Selecting the right savings account is crucial for maximising the benefits of your saved money. Here are some factors to consider:

1. Interest Rates

The interest rate offered by a savings account determines how much your money will grow over time. Look for accounts with competitive rates. Online banks often offer higher interest rates compared to traditional brick-and-mortar banks due to lower overhead costs.

2. Fees

Be aware of any fees associated with the savings account. Common fees include monthly maintenance fees, minimum balance fees, and withdrawal fees. Choose an account with low or no fees to ensure that your savings are not eroded by unnecessary charges.

3. Accessibility

Consider how easily you can access your funds. Some accounts offer online and mobile banking options, making it convenient to manage your savings from anywhere. However, ensure there are no penalties for accessing your money when needed.

4. Minimum Balance Requirements

Some savings accounts require a minimum balance to avoid fees or earn the advertised interest rate. Ensure that you can meet these requirements consistently to avoid penalties.

5. Account Type

Different types of savings accounts offer various features and benefits:

- Traditional Savings Account: These accounts are offered by most banks and credit unions and typically provide lower interest rates but high liquidity.
- High-Yield Savings Account: Offered primarily by online banks, these accounts provide higher interest rates than traditional savings accounts, making them ideal for growing your savings faster.
- Money Market Account: These accounts usually offer higher interest rates than traditional savings accounts and may come with check-writing privileges. They often require a higher minimum balance.

- Certificate of Deposit (CD): A CD offers a fixed interest rate for a specified term, ranging from a few months to several years. It typically offers higher interest rates but limits access to your funds until the term ends without penalties.

6. Security

Ensure that the savings account is insured by the Federal Deposit Insurance Corporation (FDIC) or the National Credit Union Administration (NCUA) up to the legal limit (typically $250,000 per depositor, per institution). This guarantees that your money is safe even if the bank or credit union fails.

7. Additional Features

Some savings accounts offer additional features such as automatic transfers, mobile check deposits, and integration with budgeting tools. These features can enhance the convenience and functionality of managing your savings.

Conclusion

Saving early and choosing the right savings account are essential steps toward achieving financial security and independence. By understanding the power of compound interest and selecting an account that aligns with your financial needs and goals, you can maximise the growth and safety of your savings. Building the habit of saving early not only provides a financial cushion but also sets the stage for long-term financial success and stability.

Investing 101

Investing is a powerful way to grow your wealth over time. For teenagers, learning the basics of investing early can set the foundation for a lifetime of financial stability and growth. This section will cover the basics of investing and introduce some simple investment options for teenagers.

Basics of Investing

1. What is Investing?

Investing involves putting money into financial assets with the expectation of earning a return or profit over time. Unlike saving, which focuses on preserving capital, investing aims to grow your money by taking on some level of risk.

2. Why Invest?

- Wealth Accumulation: Investing can significantly increase your wealth over time, thanks to the power of compound interest.
- Beat Inflation: Inflation erodes the purchasing power of money. Investing helps your money grow faster than the rate of inflation.
- Financial Goals: Investing can help you achieve long-term financial goals, such as buying a house, funding education, or retiring comfortably.

3. Key Investment Concepts

- Risk and Return: Higher potential returns usually come with higher risks. Understanding your risk tolerance is crucial in choosing the right investments.
- Diversification: Spreading your investments across different asset classes and sectors to reduce risk.
- Compound Interest: Earning interest on both your initial investment and the accumulated interest over time.

4. Types of Investments

- Stocks: Shares of ownership in a company. Stocks offer the potential for high returns but come with higher risk.
- Bonds: Loans made to corporations or governments in exchange for periodic interest payments and the return of the bond's face value at maturity. Bonds are generally less risky than stocks.
- Mutual Funds and ETFs: Pooled funds from multiple investors used to invest in a diversified portfolio of stocks, bonds, or other assets. These provide diversification and professional management.
- Real Estate: Property investments that can generate rental income and appreciate over time.
- Savings Accounts and CDs: Low-risk, low-return investments that are best for short-term savings.

Simple Investment Options for teenagers

1. Savings Accounts and CDs

- Savings Accounts: These are low-risk accounts that earn interest on your deposited money. They are suitable for emergency funds and short-term savings.
- Certificates of Deposit (CDs): Time deposits with higher interest rates than savings accounts. Your money is locked in for a fixed term, and early withdrawal may result in penalties.

2. Stocks

Investing in individual stocks can be exciting but requires research and understanding of the market. Here's how teenagers can start:

- Stock Market Basics: Learn about how the stock market works, different stock exchanges, and key stock market indices like the S&P 500 and the Dow Jones Industrial Average.
- Research: Look into companies, understand their business models, financial health, and growth potential.
- Brokerage Accounts: Open a brokerage account with a platform that allows teen investing with parental supervision, such as Fidelity's Youth Account or Stockpile.

3. Exchange-Traded Funds (ETFs)

ETFs are a great way to gain exposure to a broad range of stocks or bonds with a single investment. They offer diversification and lower risk compared to individual stocks. teenagers can invest in ETFs through a brokerage account.

- Types of ETFs: Understand different types of ETFs, such as equity ETFs, bond ETFs, and sector-specific ETFs.
- Benefits: Lower expense ratios, diversification, and ease of trading.

4. Mutual Funds

Mutual funds pool money from multiple investors to invest in a diversified portfolio of stocks, bonds, or other securities. They are managed by professional fund managers.

- Access: Many mutual funds have minimum investment requirements, but some accounts geared towards young investors have lower thresholds.
- Growth and Income Funds: Look for funds that balance potential growth with income generation.

5. Robo-Advisors

Robo-advisors are automated platforms that create and manage a diversified investment portfolio based on your risk tolerance and financial goals. They are an excellent option for beginners who want a hands-off approach to investing.

- Popular Platforms: Examples include Betterment, Wealthfront, and Acorns.
- Benefits: Low fees, automated rebalancing, and personalised portfolios.

6. Custodial Accounts

Custodial accounts, such as UTMA (Uniform Transfers to Minors Act) or UGMA (Uniform Gifts to Minors Act) accounts, allow parents to invest on behalf of their children. The assets in these accounts transfer to the teen once they reach adulthood.

- Investment Options: Stocks, bonds, mutual funds, and ETFs.
- Management: Parents manage the account until the child reaches the age of majority.

7. Education Savings Accounts

- 529 Plans: Tax-advantaged savings plans designed to encourage saving for future education costs. Investments grow tax-free, and withdrawals for qualified education expenses are tax-free.

- Coverdell Education Savings Account (ESA): Another tax-advantaged account for education expenses, with more investment options but lower contribution limits compared to 529 plans.

8. Micro-Investing Apps

Micro-investing apps allow teenagers to start investing with very small amounts of money. These apps are designed to make investing accessible and easy to understand.

- Acorns: Rounds up your purchases to the nearest dollar and invests the spare change.
- Stash: Allows you to invest in fractional shares of stocks and ETFs with as little as $5.

Conclusion

Understanding the basics of investing and exploring simple investment options can set teenagers on the path to financial independence and wealth accumulation. By starting early and making informed decisions, teenagers can take advantage of the power of compound interest, diversify their investments, and work towards their financial goals. Investing can be a lifelong journey, and the knowledge and habits developed now will pay dividends in the future.

Managing Money Wisely

Managing money wisely is crucial for financial stability and independence. This involves avoiding debt, understanding credit, and practising responsible spending. Here, we'll discuss these aspects in detail.

Avoiding Debt and Understanding Credit

1. Understanding Credit

Credit is essentially borrowed money that you can use to purchase goods and services when you need them, with the agreement to pay back the amount borrowed along with any applicable interest. Understanding how credit works is vital for managing debt and maintaining a healthy financial profile.

- Credit Score: This is a numerical representation of your creditworthiness. It ranges from 300 to 850, with higher scores indicating better credit health. A good credit score can help you secure loans with favourable terms.
- Credit Report: This is a detailed record of your credit history, including loans, credit cards, and payment history. Regularly reviewing your credit report can help you identify and correct errors that might affect your credit score.

2. Types of Debt

- Secured Debt: Loans that are backed by collateral, such as a mortgage or car loan. If you fail to repay the loan, the lender can seize the collateral.
- Unsecured Debt: Loans that are not backed by collateral, such as credit cards and personal loans. These typically come with higher interest rates due to the increased risk to lenders.

3. Avoiding Debt

Avoiding excessive debt is crucial for financial health. Here are some strategies:

- Budgeting: Create a budget to track your income and expenses. This helps you live within your means and avoid unnecessary debt.
- Emergency Fund: Establish an emergency fund to cover unexpected expenses, such as medical bills or car repairs, so you don't have to rely on credit.
- Paying Off Debt: Prioritise paying off high-interest debt first. Consider using the snowball method (paying off small debts first) or the avalanche method (paying off high-interest debts first).

4. Responsible Use of Credit Cards

Credit cards can be useful tools if used responsibly. Here are some tips:

- Pay in Full: Try to pay off your balance in full each month to avoid interest charges.
- Keep Utilisation Low: Aim to use less than 30% of your available credit to maintain a good credit score.
- Monitor Statements: Regularly review your credit card statements for errors and unauthorised charges.

5. Understanding Interest Rates

Interest rates significantly affect the cost of borrowing. Knowing the difference between fixed and variable interest rates, as well as the impact of compounding interest, can help you make informed borrowing decisions.

Tips for Responsible Spending

1. Create a Budget

A budget is a financial plan that helps you manage your income, expenses, and savings. Here's how to create an effective budget:

- Track Your Income: Record all sources of income, including wages, allowances, and any side gigs.
- List Your Expenses: Categorize your expenses into fixed (rent, utilities) and variable (entertainment, dining out).
- Set Savings Goals: Allocate a portion of your income to savings and investments.
- Review and Adjust: Regularly review your budget and make adjustments as needed to stay on track.

2. Differentiate Between Needs and Wants

Understanding the difference between needs and wants is crucial for responsible spending:

- Needs: Essential items and services required for survival and basic well-being, such as food, shelter, and healthcare.
- Wants: Non-essential items and services that enhance your lifestyle, such as dining out, entertainment, and luxury items.

Prioritise spending on needs before allocating money to wants.

3. Use Cash or Debit Cards

Using cash or debit cards for everyday purchases can help you stay within your budget and avoid accumulating credit card debt. This approach encourages mindful spending and reduces the temptation to overspend.

4. Plan Major Purchases

For significant expenses, such as electronics or vacations, plan ahead and save up rather than relying on credit. Research and compare prices to ensure you get the best deal.

5. Take Advantage of Discounts and Deals

Look for discounts, coupons, and sales to save money on necessary purchases. Loyalty programs and cashback apps can also help you save money on regular expenses.

6. Avoid Impulse Buying

Impulse buying can quickly derail your budget. To avoid it:

- Wait Before Buying: Implement a waiting period (e.g., 24 hours) before making non-essential purchases.
- Make a Shopping List: Stick to a shopping list to avoid buying items you don't need.
- Avoid Shopping When Emotional: Emotional states can influence spending behaviour. Shop with a clear mind.

7. Educate Yourself

Financial literacy is key to managing money wisely. Educate yourself on personal finance topics through books, online courses, and financial blogs. Knowledge empowers you to make informed financial decisions.

Conclusion

Managing money wisely involves understanding credit, avoiding excessive debt, and practising responsible spending habits. By creating a budget, prioritising needs over wants, using cash or debit cards, planning major purchases, taking advantage of discounts, avoiding impulse buying, and educating yourself on personal finance, you can build a strong financial foundation. These practices will help you achieve financial stability, reduce stress, and work towards your long-term financial goals.

Financial Tools and Apps: Best Apps for Budgeting and Saving

In today's digital age, managing finances has become easier and more accessible than ever before, thanks to a plethora of apps designed to help individuals budget, save, and track their money effectively. Whether you're looking to get a handle on daily expenses, save for a major purchase, or plan for retirement, there's a financial app out there to suit your needs. Here, we explore some of the top apps that can assist you in budgeting and saving wisely.

1. Mint

Mint is a comprehensive budgeting and financial tracking app owned by Intuit, the makers of TurboTax and QuickBooks. It allows users to link their bank accounts, credit cards, and bills in one place, providing a clear overview of their financial health. Mint categorizes transactions automatically, creating budgets based on spending patterns. It sends alerts for upcoming bills and helps users stay on track with their financial goals through personalised tips.

2. YNAB (You Need A Budget)

YNAB is based on the principle of giving every dollar a job. It focuses on zero-based budgeting, where every dollar you earn is allocated to a specific category, such as groceries, rent, or savings. YNAB syncs with bank accounts and credit cards to import transactions, encourages users to set financial goals, and provides educational resources to improve money management skills.

3. Personal Capital

Personal Capital is geared towards investors and individuals with complex financial situations. It offers tools to track investments, retirement accounts, and net worth alongside budgeting features. Personal

Capital provides insights into portfolio performance, retirement planning, and asset allocation, making it ideal for those looking to manage both daily finances and long-term investments in one place.

4. PocketGuard

PocketGuard focuses on simplifying budgeting by calculating how much disposable income you have after accounting for bills, savings goals, and spending habits. It categorises expenses, sets limits for each category, and alerts users when they are approaching their budget limits. PocketGuard's goal is to help users optimise their spending and save more efficiently without the complexity of detailed financial reports.

5. Acorns

Acorns combines budgeting with investment by automatically investing spare change from everyday purchases into a diversified portfolio. It rounds up each transaction to the nearest dollar and invests the difference in low-cost ETFs. Acorns also offers retirement account options, education savings plans, and tools to set financial goals based on individual preferences and risk tolerance.

6. Simple

Simple is a mobile banking app that integrates budgeting and banking features. It offers a fee-free checking account with budgeting tools such as savings goals, expense tracking, and automated categorization of transactions. Simple's goal is to provide a seamless banking experience while helping users manage their money more effectively through visual representations of their financial habits.

7. Goodbudget

Goodbudget operates on the envelope budgeting system, where users allocate funds to virtual envelopes for different spending categories, such as groceries, utilities, and entertainment. It promotes conscious spending by limiting expenditures to the amount available in each envelope. Goodbudget syncs across multiple devices and allows for sharing budgets with family members, making it suitable for households aiming to manage finances collectively.

8. Clarity Money

Clarity Money focuses on cancelling and managing subscriptions, lowering bills, and tracking spending to improve financial health. It analyses transactions to identify recurring payments and subscriptions that users may want to cancel or renegotiate. Clarity Money also provides insights into spending habits and suggests ways to save money based on personalized recommendations.

9. Honeyfi

Honeyfi is designed for couples to manage finances together. It allows partners to create budgets, track expenses, and set savings goals collaboratively. Honeyfi syncs bank accounts and credit cards to provide real-time updates on joint financial activities. It also facilitates communication about money matters through chat features and notifications, promoting transparency and teamwork in financial planning.

10. Wally

Wally offers expense tracking and budgeting tools aimed at simplicity and clarity. It allows users to set savings goals, categorize expenses, and visualize spending patterns through customizable reports and graphs. Wally supports multiple currencies and integrates with location services to track spending habits based on geographical locations. Its minimalist design appeals to users looking for straightforward budgeting solutions without unnecessary complexities.

Using Technology to Track Finances

The advent of smartphones and mobile apps has revolutionised how individuals track and manage their finances. These technologies not only provide convenience but also empower users with real-time insights into their financial habits, helping them make informed decisions to achieve their financial goals. Here are some ways technology has transformed financial tracking:

1. Real-Time Updates

Financial apps sync with bank accounts and credit cards to provide real-time updates on transactions and account balances. This instant access to financial information enables users to monitor their spending habits closely and identify areas where they can cut costs or redirect funds towards savings goals.

2. Automation

Automation features in financial apps streamline repetitive tasks such as bill payments, savings transfers, and investment contributions. Users can set up recurring transactions and savings goals, allowing them to stay on track with their financial plans without manual intervention.

3. Customization and Personalization

Financial apps offer customizable budgeting tools that cater to individual preferences and financial goals. Users can create personalised budgets, set spending limits for different categories, and receive notifications when they exceed predefined limits. This customization helps users adapt their financial strategies to changing circumstances and priorities.

4. Financial Education

Many financial apps include educational resources and tips to improve money management skills. They provide insights into budgeting techniques, investment strategies, and debt management, empowering users to make informed financial decisions and build long-term financial stability.

5. Security and Privacy

Technology has enhanced the security measures implemented by financial institutions and apps to protect users' sensitive information. Encryption, multi-factor authentication, and biometric verification methods ensure that financial data remains secure and private, giving users peace of mind when using digital financial services.

6. Integration with Other Services

Financial apps often integrate with other services such as tax preparation software, investment platforms, and banking institutions. This integration allows users to manage all aspects of their financial lives from a single platform, simplifying financial management and improving overall efficiency.

7. Behavioural Insights

Advanced analytics and data visualisation tools in financial apps provide behavioural insights into spending patterns and financial habits. Users can analyse trends, identify areas for improvement, and make proactive adjustments to achieve their financial goals more effectively.

8. Accessibility

Mobile accessibility ensures that users can manage their finances anytime, anywhere, using their smartphones or tablets. This accessibility promotes financial awareness and accountability, empowering users to stay engaged with their financial goals on the go.

In conclusion, financial tools and apps have democratised access to effective budgeting, saving, and financial tracking tools. Whether you're a seasoned investor or just starting to manage your finances, there's a wide range of apps available to help you achieve financial success and stability. By leveraging technology, individuals can take control of their financial futures and build a solid foundation for long-term financial health.

Making Your Money Grow: Compound Interest Explained and Long-Term Investment Strategies

Building wealth and making your money grow over time requires understanding fundamental concepts like compound interest and employing effective long-term investment strategies. Whether you're saving for retirement, a major purchase, or financial independence, these principles play a crucial role in achieving your financial goals.

Compound Interest Explained

Compound interest is often referred to as the "eighth wonder of the world" for its powerful ability to exponentially increase wealth over time. Unlike simple interest, which only calculates interest on the principal amount, compound interest takes into account both the initial principal and the accumulated interest from previous periods.

Here's how compound interest works:

1. Initial Principle: Suppose you invest $1,000 at an annual interest rate of 5%.

2. First Year: At the end of the first year, your investment grows by 5%, earning you $50 in interest. Your total becomes $1,050.

3. Subsequent Years: In the second year, you earn interest not only on the initial $1,000 but also on the $50 interest earned in the first year. So, at 5% interest, you earn $52.50, bringing your total to $1,102.50.

4. Long-Term Growth: Over longer periods, compound interest continues to accelerate your earnings. The key to maximising its benefits is time—the longer your money compounds, the more substantial the growth.

Compound interest can be calculated using the formula:

$$A = P \left(1 + \frac{r}{n}\right)^{nt}$$

Where:
- A is the amount of money accumulated after n years, including interest.
- P is the principal amount (initial investment).
- r is the annual interest rate (decimal).
- n is the number of times that interest is compounded per year.
- t is the number of years the money is invested for.

For example, if you invest $1,000 at an annual interest rate of 5% compounded annually for 10 years:

$$A = 1000 \left(1 + \frac{0.05}{1}\right)^{1 \cdot 10} = 1000 \times (1.05)^{10} \approx \$1,628.89$$

This example illustrates how compound interest can significantly increase your initial investment over time.

Long-Term Investment Strategies

While understanding compound interest is essential, effective long-term investment strategies are equally crucial for achieving financial growth and security. Here are some key strategies to consider:

1. Start Early and Stay Consistent: The power of compounding works best over long periods. Start investing early to take advantage of time, even if you can only invest small amounts initially. Consistently contribute to your investments to harness the benefits of dollar-cost averaging.

2. Diversification: Spread your investments across different asset classes, industries, and geographical regions to reduce risk. Diversification helps mitigate losses in one area by potentially gaining in another, balancing your portfolio's overall performance.

3. Invest for the Long Term: Long-term investments, such as stocks and bonds, historically yield higher returns than short-term investments. While they may be more volatile in the short term, they tend to outperform over extended periods, especially when considering inflation and economic growth.

4. Retirement Accounts: Maximise contributions to tax-advantaged retirement accounts like 401(k)s or IRAs. These accounts offer tax benefits and compound growth opportunities, allowing your investments to grow faster compared to taxable accounts.

5. Rebalance Your Portfolio: Regularly review and rebalance your investment portfolio to maintain your desired asset allocation. Rebalancing ensures that your risk level remains in line with your financial goals and helps you capitalize on opportunities as market conditions change.

6. Educate Yourself: Stay informed about financial markets, investment trends, and economic factors that impact your investments. Continuously educate yourself to make informed decisions and adjust your strategies as needed.

7. Consider Risk Tolerance and Goals: Your risk tolerance and financial goals should guide your investment decisions. A younger investor with a longer time horizon may tolerate higher risk for potentially higher returns, while someone closer to retirement may prioritise capital preservation.

8. Seek Professional Advice: If you're unsure about investment strategies or navigating financial markets, consider consulting with a financial advisor. An advisor can provide personalised guidance based on your financial situation, goals, and risk tolerance.

9. Monitor and Adjust: Regularly monitor your investments and adjust your strategy as necessary. Market conditions, economic factors, and personal circumstances may warrant changes to your asset allocation or investment selections over time.

Conclusion

Making your money grow requires patience, discipline, and a sound understanding of financial principles like compound interest and long-term investment strategies. By harnessing the power of compound interest and implementing effective investment strategies, you can build wealth, achieve financial goals, and secure your financial future. Start early, stay informed, diversify your investments, and seek professional advice when needed to maximise your potential for long-term financial success. Remember, the journey to financial independence begins with informed decisions and a commitment to long-term wealth building.

The Importance of Financial Literacy

Resources for Continued Learning and How Financial Knowledge Impacts Life Decisions

Financial literacy is the ability to understand and effectively apply various financial skills, including personal financial management, budgeting, investing, and debt management. It empowers individuals to make informed financial decisions, plan for the future, and achieve financial security. In today's complex financial landscape, possessing financial literacy is more crucial than ever. Here's why it matters and how it can impact life decisions:

Resources for Continued Learning

Continued learning is essential for improving financial literacy and staying updated with financial trends and strategies. Fortunately, there are numerous resources available to enhance financial knowledge:

1. Online Courses and Webinars: Platforms like Coursera, edX, and Udemy offer courses on personal finance, investing, retirement planning, and more. These courses are often taught by industry experts and allow learners to study at their own pace.

2. Books and Publications: Books authored by financial experts provide comprehensive insights into various aspects of finance. Popular titles include "The Intelligent Investor" by Benjamin Graham, "Rich Dad Poor Dad" by Robert Kiyosaki, and "The Total Money Makeover" by Dave Ramsey.

3. Financial Blogs and Websites: Blogs such as The Financial Diet, Mr. Money Mustache, and The Simple Dollar offer practical tips, personal finance stories, and advice on managing money effectively.

4. Podcasts: Podcasts like "The Dave Ramsey Show," "Afford Anything," and "Planet Money" cover a wide range of financial topics, providing listeners with valuable information and advice in an accessible format.

5. Financial Advisors and Consultants: Consulting with a certified financial planner (CFP) or financial advisor can provide personalised guidance tailored to individual financial goals and circumstances.

6. Government and Nonprofit Resources: Organisations like the Consumer Financial Protection Bureau (CFPB) and nonprofit institutions often offer free resources, workshops, and tools to improve financial literacy among the public.

7. Financial Literacy Programs: Many educational institutions and community organisations offer workshops and seminars on financial literacy, aimed at teaching basic financial concepts and practical money management skills.

How Financial Knowledge Impacts Life Decisions

Financial literacy influences various aspects of life decisions, ranging from daily budgeting to long-term financial planning and beyond:

1. Personal Finance Management: Individuals with financial literacy skills can effectively manage their income, expenses, and savings. They understand the importance of budgeting, avoiding debt, and building emergency funds to withstand financial challenges.

2. Investment Decisions: Financially literate individuals can make informed decisions about investing in stocks, bonds, mutual funds, and other assets. They understand risk tolerance, asset allocation, and the potential returns and risks associated with different investment options.

3. Debt Management: Knowledge of debt management strategies helps individuals avoid high-interest debt, repay loans efficiently, and improve their credit scores. Financially literate individuals are less likely to fall into debt traps and understand the implications of borrowing money.

4. Retirement Planning: Understanding retirement planning principles allows individuals to set realistic retirement goals, contribute to retirement accounts like 401(k)s and IRAs, and make informed decisions about Social Security benefits and pension plans.

5. Major Purchases: Whether buying a home, car, or funding higher education, financial literacy helps individuals evaluate financing options, negotiate terms, and make decisions that align with their long-term financial goals.

6. Entrepreneurship and Business Ventures: Entrepreneurs and small business owners benefit from financial literacy by managing cash flow, understanding financial statements, securing financing, and making strategic business decisions.

7. Financial Security and Well-Being: Ultimately, financial literacy contributes to overall financial security and well-being. It reduces stress related to money management, enhances financial independence, and allows individuals to achieve their desired lifestyle and future aspirations.

Conclusion

Financial literacy is not just about understanding numbers; it's about empowering individuals to make informed decisions that positively impact their financial well-being and future prospects. By continuously learning and applying financial knowledge, individuals can navigate today's complex financial landscape with confidence, build wealth, and achieve their financial goals. Accessing resources for continued learning and understanding how financial knowledge influences life decisions are key steps toward improving financial literacy and securing a stable financial future. Whether through self-study, professional advice, or educational programs, investing in financial literacy pays dividends in both the short and long term.

Dealing with Financial Challenges

Overcoming Financial Setbacks and Learning from Mistakes

Financial challenges are a common part of life for many individuals and families. Whether caused by unexpected expenses, job loss, poor financial decisions, or economic downturns, facing financial setbacks can be daunting. However, overcoming these challenges and learning from mistakes can lead to valuable lessons and improved financial resilience. Here's how to navigate through financial difficulties:

Overcoming Financial Setbacks

1. Assess the Situation: When faced with a financial setback, such as a sudden expense or loss of income, take time to assess your current financial situation. Review your income, expenses, savings, and debts to understand the extent of the setback and identify areas where adjustments can be made.

2. Create a Budget and Prioritize Expenses: Develop a realistic budget that aligns with your current financial circumstances. Prioritize essential expenses such as housing, utilities, food, and healthcare. Cut back on discretionary spending and non-essential purchases to conserve funds during challenging times.

3. Explore Additional Income Sources: Consider temporary or part-time work, freelance opportunities, or selling unused items to generate additional income. Diversifying income streams can provide financial stability and offset temporary financial setbacks.

4. Negotiate with Creditors and Service Providers: If you're struggling to meet financial obligations, communicate with creditors, landlords, or service providers proactively. Negotiate repayment plans, deferment options, or reduced payment arrangements to alleviate financial pressure and avoid defaulting on payments.

5. Utilise Emergency Savings: If you have an emergency fund or savings account, use it to cover essential expenses and bridge temporary gaps in income. If you don't have an emergency fund, prioritise building one as part of your long-term financial planning strategy.

6. Seek Financial Assistance and Support: Research available financial assistance programs, government benefits, or community resources that may provide temporary relief or financial aid during challenging times. Seek guidance from financial advisors or nonprofit organisations specialising in financial counselling.

7. Stay Positive and Maintain Perspective: Dealing with financial setbacks can be stressful and emotionally draining. Maintain a positive mindset, focus on practical solutions, and remind yourself that setbacks are temporary challenges that can be overcome with perseverance and determination.

Learning from Mistakes

1. Reflect on Financial Decisions: Take time to reflect on the circumstances and decisions that led to the financial setback. Identify any mistakes, oversights, or behavioral patterns that contributed to the situation. Honest self-reflection is crucial for learning and growth.

2. Understand Root Causes: Determine the root causes of financial mistakes or missteps. Whether it was overspending, inadequate savings, excessive debt, or lack of financial planning, understanding the underlying factors can help prevent similar issues in the future.

3. Adjust Financial Habits and Behaviours: Use insights gained from past mistakes to adjust your financial habits and behaviours. Develop a disciplined approach to budgeting, saving, and spending that aligns with your financial goals and priorities. Implement strategies to avoid impulsive or emotional financial decisions.

4. Educate Yourself: Increase your financial literacy by learning about personal finance topics, investment strategies, debt management techniques, and effective budgeting practices. Stay informed about economic trends, consumer rights, and financial regulations that may impact your financial decisions.

5. Seek Professional Guidance: If you're unsure how to address specific financial challenges or improve financial habits, consider consulting with a financial advisor or counsellor. A professional can provide personalised guidance, identify opportunities for improvement, and help you develop a strategic plan for financial success.

6. Build Resilience and Preparedness: Use the lessons learned from past financial setbacks to build resilience and preparedness for future challenges. Maintain an emergency fund, review and update your financial plan regularly, and take proactive steps to protect your financial well-being against unforeseen events.

7. Share Knowledge and Support Others: Share your experiences and lessons learned with family members, friends, or colleagues who may benefit from your insights. Offer support and encouragement to others facing similar financial challenges, fostering a sense of community and mutual learning.

Conclusion

Dealing with financial challenges requires resilience, resourcefulness, and a proactive approach to overcoming setbacks and learning from mistakes. By assessing your situation, creating a budget, exploring additional income sources, and seeking support when needed, you can navigate through financial difficulties with confidence and determination. Learning from past mistakes, adjusting financial behaviours, and continuously educating yourself are essential steps toward building financial resilience and achieving long-term financial stability. Remember, each challenge presents an opportunity for growth and improvement on your journey toward financial well-being.

Planning for the Future

College Savings Plans and Preparing for Major Life Expenses

Planning for the future involves anticipating and preparing for significant life events and expenses, such as funding higher education and managing other major financial obligations. By proactively strategizing and implementing savings plans, individuals and families can navigate these milestones with financial confidence and security.

College Savings Plans

Saving for college education is a substantial financial goal for many families. Rising tuition costs and expenses associated with higher education necessitate early planning and disciplined savings strategies. Here are common college savings plans to consider:

1. 529 College Savings Plans: A 529 plan is a tax-advantaged investment account designed specifically for saving for future college costs. Contributions grow tax-deferred, and withdrawals used for qualified education expenses are tax-free at the federal level. Many states also offer tax benefits for residents contributing to their state's 529 plan. These plans typically offer investment options ranging from conservative to aggressive portfolios.

2. Coverdell Education Savings Accounts (ESA): Coverdell ESAs are another tax-advantaged option for saving for education expenses, including elementary, secondary, and higher education costs. Contributions are not tax-deductible, but earnings grow tax-free, and withdrawals are tax-free when used for qualified education expenses.

3. Prepaid Tuition Plans: Some states offer prepaid tuition plans that allow families to purchase future college tuition credits at today's prices. These plans can help hedge against tuition inflation, providing certainty about future education costs. However, they may be limited to in-state public universities or have restrictions on usage.

4. Roth IRA: While primarily used for retirement savings, a Roth IRA can also serve as a flexible option for college savings. Contributions can be withdrawn penalty-free for qualified education expenses, although earnings may be subject to taxes and penalties if withdrawn early. Roth IRAs offer investment flexibility and tax-free growth potential.

5. Traditional Savings Accounts and Investments: Traditional savings accounts, CDs (Certificates of Deposit), and taxable investment accounts are straightforward options for saving for college. While they lack the tax advantages of dedicated college savings plans, they offer flexibility and liquidity.

6. Scholarships, Grants, and Financial Aid: Encourage your child to apply for scholarships and grants to help offset college costs. Completing the Free Application for Federal Student Aid (FAFSA) can also determine eligibility for federal and state financial aid programs, including grants, loans, and work-study opportunities.

Preparing for Major Life Expenses

In addition to college savings, preparing for other major life expenses requires careful financial planning and preparation. Here are key considerations and strategies:

1. Homeownership: Saving for a down payment, closing costs, and ongoing homeownership expenses (e.g., property taxes, maintenance) is crucial for prospective homebuyers. Evaluate mortgage options,

improve credit scores, and budget for homeownership expenses to achieve homeownership goals responsibly.

2. Weddings and Celebrations: Budgeting for weddings, anniversaries, and other celebrations involves estimating costs, setting priorities, and saving accordingly. Consider alternative venues, DIY projects, and guest list management to control expenses without compromising celebration quality.

3. Emergency Funds: Building and maintaining an emergency fund is essential for covering unexpected expenses, such as medical emergencies, car repairs, or job loss. Aim to save three to six months' worth of living expenses in a liquid savings account to provide financial security during challenging times.

4. Retirement Planning: While not an immediate expense, planning for retirement is a long-term financial goal that requires consistent saving and investment. Maximise contributions to retirement accounts, such as 401(k)s and IRAs, take advantage of employer matching contributions, and review investment strategies regularly to achieve retirement readiness.

5. Healthcare Costs: Anticipate healthcare expenses, including insurance premiums, deductibles, and out-of-pocket costs for medical care. Consider health savings accounts (HSAs) for tax-advantaged savings and flexible spending accounts (FSAs) for eligible medical expenses.

6. Travel and Leisure: Budgeting for vacations, travel experiences, and leisure activities requires balancing enjoyment with financial prudence. Plan and save for travel expenses, explore travel rewards programs, and prioritise experiences that align with your budget and financial goals.

Conclusion

Planning for the future involves preparing for significant life events and expenses through disciplined savings, strategic investment, and informed decision-making. Whether saving for college education, homeownership, retirement, or other major life milestones, proactive financial planning enhances financial security and enables individuals and families to achieve their long-term goals. By leveraging tax-advantaged savings plans, diversifying investments, and prioritising savings goals, individuals can navigate life's financial challenges with confidence and build a solid foundation for future success. Start early, stay informed, and adjust strategies as needed to ensure financial readiness and resilience in pursuing your aspirations and securing your financial future.

Giving Back

The Role of Charity and Philanthropy, and How to Make a Positive Impact with Your Money

Giving back through charity and philanthropy plays a crucial role in society by addressing social issues, supporting communities in need, and promoting positive change. Whether through financial contributions, volunteerism, or advocacy, individuals can make a meaningful impact and contribute to the greater good. Here's a look at the significance of charity and philanthropy, and strategies for making a positive impact with your money:

The Role of Charity and Philanthropy

1. Addressing Social Issues: Charitable organisations and philanthropic initiatives play a vital role in addressing social issues such as poverty, hunger, education inequality, healthcare access, environmental conservation, and more. They provide essential services, advocacy efforts, and resources to improve quality of life and create lasting societal change.

2. Supporting Communities in Need: Charitable giving supports vulnerable populations, including disadvantaged communities, marginalised groups, and individuals facing crises or hardships. It provides resources for basic needs, emergency relief, economic empowerment, and opportunities for personal and community development.

3. Promoting Education and Research: Philanthropy contributes to educational institutions, research organisations, and scholarship programs that advance knowledge, innovation, and intellectual growth. Funding academic research, scholarships, and educational initiatives enhances learning opportunities and fosters future leaders and innovators.

4. Advancing Healthcare and Wellness: Charitable donations to healthcare organisations, medical research, and public health initiatives improve healthcare access, advance medical treatments, and promote wellness initiatives. Philanthropy supports medical advancements, disease prevention efforts, and initiatives to improve overall community health.

5. Cultural Preservation and Arts: Supporting cultural institutions, museums, libraries, and arts organisations preserves cultural heritage, promotes artistic expression, and enriches communities through cultural experiences, exhibitions, and educational programs.

6. Environmental Conservation and Sustainability: Philanthropy plays a critical role in environmental conservation, sustainability initiatives, and efforts to combat climate change. Supporting environmental organisations, conservation projects, and eco-friendly initiatives promotes environmental stewardship and protects natural resources for future generations.

How to Make a Positive Impact with Your Money

1. Identify Causes and Organizations: Identify causes and charitable organisations that align with your values, passions, and interests. Research nonprofit organisations, charities, and philanthropic initiatives to understand their missions, impact, and financial transparency.

2. Set Giving Goals and Budget: Establish giving goals and budget allocations for charitable donations and philanthropic contributions. Determine how much you can afford to donate annually or on a regular basis while considering your financial situation and long-term financial goals.

3. Research Effective Giving Strategies: Research effective giving strategies and philanthropic approaches to maximise the impact of your donations. Consider giving to organisations with proven track records, measurable outcomes, and transparent financial practices.

4. Support Local and Global Initiatives: Support both local community initiatives and global causes to address immediate needs and broader societal issues. Consider giving locally to support grassroots organisations and initiatives that directly benefit your community.

5. Volunteer Time and Skills: In addition to financial contributions, volunteer your time, skills, and expertise to support charitable organisations and community initiatives. Participate in volunteer programs, community service projects, and advocacy efforts to make a hands-on impact.

6. Encourage Workplace Giving and Matching Programs: Take advantage of workplace giving campaigns, matching gift programs, and employee volunteer opportunities offered by employers. Engage with corporate social responsibility initiatives to amplify your impact and support charitable causes collectively.

7. Plan for Long-Term Impact: Consider legacy giving and planned giving strategies to support charitable organisations and causes beyond your lifetime. Explore options such as bequests, charitable trusts, and endowments to create lasting impact and support future generations.

Conclusion

Giving back through charity and philanthropy empowers individuals to make a positive difference in their communities and the world at large. By supporting charitable organisations, addressing social issues, and promoting positive change, individuals can contribute to a more equitable, compassionate, and sustainable society. Whether through financial contributions, volunteerism, or advocacy, each act of giving contributes to collective efforts to improve lives, strengthen communities, and build a brighter future for all. Embrace the opportunity to give back, leverage your resources for meaningful impact, and inspire others to join in creating positive change through charitable giving and philanthropic endeavours.

Case Studies and Real-Life Examples

Success Stories of Financially Savvy teenagers and Learning from Real-Life Scenarios

Real-life examples and case studies of financially savvy teenagers provide valuable insights into effective financial practices, lessons learned from challenges, and strategies for achieving financial success at a young age. By examining these success stories and real-life scenarios, individuals can glean practical tips, inspiration, and actionable strategies for improving their own financial literacy and decision-making skills.

Success Stories of Financially Savvy teenagers

1. Teen Entrepreneurs: Many financially savvy teenagers demonstrate entrepreneurial spirit by launching successful businesses or ventures. For example, a teen may start a small online business selling handmade crafts, digital services, or niche products, leveraging e-commerce platforms and social media for marketing and sales.

2. Budgeting and Saving: teenagers who excel in budgeting and saving demonstrate disciplined financial habits from a young age. For instance, a teen may allocate a portion of their earnings from part-time jobs or allowances toward savings goals, such as college tuition, a car, or future investments.

3. Investment and Financial Literacy: Some teenagers exhibit advanced financial literacy by investing in stocks, bonds, or mutual funds through custodial accounts or educational resources. Learning about investment strategies, risk management, and market trends enables teenagers to build wealth and prepare for future financial goals.

4. Financial Education Advocates: Financially savvy teenagers may actively promote financial education and literacy among their peers and communities. They participate in school clubs,

workshops, or volunteer initiatives focused on teaching basic money management skills, budgeting techniques, and responsible financial behaviours.

5. Scholarship and College Planning: teenagers who excel in academics and extracurricular activities often secure scholarships and financial aid for higher education. They research scholarship opportunities, maintain strong academic records, and engage in community service to enhance their college applications and financial prospects.

Learning from Real-Life Scenarios

1. Managing Debt and Credit: Real-life scenarios illustrate the consequences of mismanaging debt and credit. For instance, a teen may learn about the importance of maintaining a good credit score, avoiding high-interest debt, and responsibly using credit cards through personal experiences or family discussions.

2. Emergency Fund Preparation: Learning from real-life scenarios involves preparing for unexpected expenses or emergencies. A teen may witness the impact of having an emergency fund, accessing savings for unforeseen medical bills or car repairs, and the value of financial preparedness.

3. Family Financial Discussions: teenagers benefit from family discussions about financial goals, budgeting strategies, and household expenses. Real-life scenarios encourage open communication about money management, financial priorities, and collaborative decision-making within the family unit.

4. Career Planning and Income Management: teenagers explore career planning and income management through real-life scenarios, such as job interviews, internships, and part-time

employment. They learn about negotiating salaries, budgeting income, and aligning career aspirations with financial goals.

5. Long-Term Financial Planning: Real-life scenarios prompt discussions about long-term financial planning, including retirement savings, investments, and financial independence. teenagers gain insights into setting financial goals, making informed decisions, and building a secure financial future.

Conclusion

Examining success stories of financially savvy teenagers and learning from real-life scenarios provides valuable lessons and inspiration for improving financial literacy and decision-making skills at a young age. By exploring entrepreneurial endeavours, budgeting techniques, investment strategies, and responsible financial behaviours, teenagers can cultivate lifelong habits for financial success and independence. Real-life examples illustrate the importance of financial education, proactive planning, and practical application of financial principles in achieving personal and professional goals. Encourage teenagers to leverage these case studies and real-life examples to empower themselves with knowledge, skills, and confidence in managing their finances effectively and responsibly throughout their lives.

Conclusion

Recap of Key Takeaways

In exploring various aspects of personal finance, from budgeting and saving to investing and philanthropy, several key takeaways emerge:

1. Financial Literacy is Empowering: Understanding financial concepts and practices empowers individuals to make informed decisions, manage resources effectively, and plan for their future financial goals.

2. Compound Interest and Long-Term Planning: Leveraging the power of compound interest through long-term investment strategies can significantly grow wealth over time. Starting early and staying consistent with savings and investments are critical to maximising financial growth.

3. Navigating Financial Challenges: Financial setbacks are inevitable, but overcoming them involves assessing the situation, adjusting financial strategies, and learning from mistakes to build resilience and financial stability.

4. Planning for Major Life Expenses: Whether saving for college, homeownership, retirement, or other significant milestones, proactive planning and disciplined savings habits are essential for achieving financial goals and preparing for life's transitions.

5. Giving Back and Making a Difference: Engaging in charitable giving and philanthropy not only supports worthy causes but also fosters a sense of community, social responsibility, and personal fulfilment.

6. Learning from Success Stories and Real-Life Scenarios: Examining success stories of financially savvy teenagers and real-life financial scenarios provides valuable insights into effective financial practices, lessons learned, and strategies for achieving financial success at any age.

Encouragement to Take Control of Your Financial Future

Taking control of your financial future begins with education, awareness, and proactive decision-making. Here are some words of encouragement:

- Educate Yourself: Continuously educate yourself about personal finance topics, investment strategies, and economic trends. Stay informed and seek out resources that enhance your financial knowledge and skills.

- Set Clear Financial Goals: Define your financial goals, whether short-term or long-term, and create a plan to achieve them. Establishing clear objectives helps you stay focused and motivated on your journey toward financial success.

- Practise Financial Discipline: Develop disciplined financial habits, such as budgeting, saving consistently, avoiding debt, and living within your means. These habits form the foundation for financial stability and resilience against economic uncertainties.

- Seek Professional Guidance When Needed: Don't hesitate to seek advice from financial advisors or counsellors to address complex financial issues, investment decisions, or major life transitions. Professional guidance can provide clarity and confidence in your financial planning.

- Embrace Financial Responsibility: Take ownership of your financial decisions and embrace responsibility for managing your money effectively. By making informed choices and prioritising financial well-being, you can shape a secure and prosperous future.

- Inspire and Support Others: Share your financial journey, insights, and knowledge with others to inspire positive financial behaviours and empower those around you to achieve their financial goals.

Conclusion

In conclusion, mastering personal finance is a journey that requires dedication, learning, and adaptability. By applying the principles of financial literacy, planning for the future, giving back to your community, and learning from both successes and setbacks, you can take control of your financial future with confidence and resilience. Empower yourself with knowledge, embrace financial responsibility, and strive towards building a secure and fulfilling life. Remember, each step you take today contributes to a brighter and more prosperous tomorrow.

www.ingramcontent.com/pod-product-compliance
Lightning Source LLC
Chambersburg PA
CBHW082240220526
45479CB00005B/1289